VICTORIAN Easter

and the

Springtime Celebrations
of a
Romantic Age

BY
DAVE CHEADLE

PREMIUM PRESS AMERICA
Nashville, Tennessee

VICTORIAN EASTER by Dave Cheadle

Published by PREMIUM PRESS AMERICA

Copyright © 2006 by Dave Cheadle

ISBN 1-887654-37-2

Library of Congress Catalog Card Number 2004097799

PREMIUM PRESS AMERICA gift books are available at special discounts for premiums, sales promotions, fund-raising, or educational use. For details contact the Publisher at P.O. Box 159015, Nashville, TN 37215, or phone toll free (800) 891-7323 or (615)256-8484, or fax (615)256-8624.

www.premiumpressamerica.com

Cover and typesetting by Bob Bubnis/BookSetters

First Edition 2006
1 2 3 4 5 6 7 8 9 10

Dedication

To the Lord of Easter:

Early on Sunday morning, as the new day was dawning, Mary Magdalene and the other Mary went out to see the tomb. Suddenly there was a great earthquake, because an angel of the Lord came down from heaven and rolled aside the stone and sat on it.

"I know you are looking for Jesus, who was crucified. He isn't here! He has been raised from the dead, just as he said would happen."

The First Easter Sunrise—Bible, Matthew 28

The Lord is risen.

Visions of Easter's Power

"Suddenly two men in clothes that gleamed like lightning stood beside them. In their fright the women bowed down with their faces to the ground, but the men said to them, 'Why do you look for the living among the dead? He is not here; he has risen!'"
Luke 24: 4, 5

For almost 2,000 years, the empty cross has represented Christ's victory over death on Easter morning. Trumpet Lilies are a much newer Easter symbol, first adopted by Victorians in the 1870s when importing them began.

Celebrations for the Soul
Faith, Hope, Joy and the Easter Vision

Easter was one of the most joyful holidays of the Victorian age. The term "Victorian" comes from the 64-year reign of Queen Victoria, but it usually refers to the period from the 1870s to about 1915, when WWI challenged old values, attitudes and styles forever.

Victorians imported Easter lilies from Japan and Bermuda.

Springtime holidays and celebrations of new life can be found in almost every culture throughout history. The Easter holiday that is enjoyed by many Americans today is actually based upon a variety of traditions spanning thousands of years and dozens of cultures from around the world. It was not until the eclectic Victorian age, during the reign of Queen Victoria (and then her son Edward), that many of these traditions came together into the collection of Easter festivities we recognize today.

HE IS RISEN!

Oh, let each flower that meets our sight

Recall the Lord of life and light.

ALLELUIA!

"*Come worship the risen Lord! Like the perfume of lilies, let the tribute of your heart ascend to heaven.*"
—A Victorian Easter card.

An angel and lilies appear as symbols of the miracle of life after death on two 1878 cards printed by Prang & Co. of Boston.

EASTER DAY!

The warbling bird in glad song heard,
The flower with incense sweet,
Proclaim the risen Lord, and cast
Their offerings at His feet!

At the heart of Victorian Easter celebrations was faith in the Bible's claim that Jesus Christ had risen from his tomb after an undeserved death upon a cross. Leonardo da Vinci's famous painting, The Last Supper, was well known by Victorians, who believed that Jesus had shared a final meal with his disciples during Passover on the night he was betrayed. Although innocent, Jesus was crucified, then three days later he returned on Easter to teach the world about forgiveness and life after death through his sacrifice.

Da Vinci's "The Last Supper," from the Bible in Luke 22:21, appears on many Easter cards.

A PEACEFUL EASTER

Victorian Easter

In most Victorian churches, a Palm Sunday service was observed the week prior to Easter. Fern fronds and palm branches were waved in the air and placed in church aisles to commemorate Christ's entry into Jerusalem during Passover.

Easter arrives each spring at the climax of Holy Week. For many Victorians, this holiday of singing, feasts, and fun provided a time of cheerful release after the bleak months of winter and the somber days of Lent. Maundy Thursday and Good Friday focused upon the Last Supper and the suffering of Jesus. Easter embraced the rejoicing of angels and disciples over the Easter vision of eternal life.

Easter Greetings

"*The Easter Carol*" *(right) was printed by the Woolson Spice Company in the spring of 1894.*

For centuries prior to the invention of electric lights, candles of different sizes and colors played important symbolic roles in worship services. On Easter Eve, many Victorians still observed much older traditions by lighting tall white "Paschal" candles in a ceremony called "striking the new fire." This ritual was partially to respect those who had abandonded the spring bonfires of ancient pagan festivals.

Victorian Easter

Easter
Greeting

A joyful celebration of religious symbols, colors and smells is captured by an Easter greeting showing an altar boy swinging a golden censer among lilies, tulips and spring blossoms.

The Lamb

One of the oldest symbols of the Christian faith is the lamb, which represents Jesus. The lamb points back thousands of years to Jewish Passovers and the Hebrew system of sacrifices. Because of his sacrificial death on the cross, Jesus was described in the Bible as "the Lamb of God who takes away the sins of the world" (John 1:29).

(Opposite) A lamb emerges from an Easter egg in order to symbolize Christ's rising from the tomb.

EASTER
GREETING

Lily of the Valley blooms hang like tiny white bells around a cross in a message that summoned Victorians to join "with the Angel throng" and to worshipfully sing "Alleluia!" on Easter morning.

Ellen Clapsaddle, one of the most prolific illustrators of the Victorian era, used purples in her Easter angel designs. Easter's purple symbolized Jesus' royalty.

Victorian Easter

A Happy Easter

The pensive beauty of stained glass windows and quiet worship was captured by a set of Easter cards showing women with flowers in church. One example depicts a Victorian favorite, the white and yellow narcissus.

Butterflies were widely cherished as symbols of new life and resurrection. This lithograph from the late 1880s preserves classic Victorian taste and sentiments, with flowers and an egg arranged upon a tasseled silk pillow.

REJOICE! 'TIS EASTERTIDE!

"GOD hath both raised up the LORD, and will also raise up us by his own power."

*Open The
window of
Thy Soul,
And cast its
cares away
When Easter
gilds The
dreaming hills,
The Shadows
flee away.*

"When Easter

gilds the

dreaming hills,

the shadows

flee away."

For added beauty and visual impact, fancy cards were often run through the presses one last time to apply gold ink highlights. This "gilding" process created cards now described as gilded or gilt. Real and fake gold leafing was so popular that Mark Twain wrote a novel set in this period that he titled, The Gilded Age.

"Open the Window of Thy Soul," reads one gilt-lettered card that was mailed to Seattle in 1912.

Easter Services on Mt. Rubidoux,
Riverside, Cal.

Easter Sunrise Worship Services and Easter Parades

EASTER SUNDAY PARADE
ATLANTIC CITY, N. J.

A century ago, Easter sunrise worship services grew popular in America.
Christians across the nation celebrated Easter morning with songs and prayers.

FIFTH AVE.
NEW YORK
EASTER SUNDAY

After morning worship, Victorians would often depart from church in their finest hats and clothes to stroll down their favorite streets. These promenades became so popular that by the turn-of-the-century they had evolved into "Easter Parades."

Easter Greetings

Egg contests, laughter, and music were enjoyed around the world during the Easter celebrations of a century ago. In 1889, John Philip Sousa's famous Marine Band performed while hundreds of children competed in "Egg Croquet" and egg races on the White House lawn.

Celebrating with Eggs
Prizes of all Colors, Styles and Sizes

Egg contests and simple events like egg stacking once delighted Victorian children in cities large and small.

Eggs have played an important role in springtime celebrations for hundreds of years. Some historians say that fancy eggs were given as gifts symbolizing fertility and new life going back to the times of ancient China, Greece and Rome.

As Christianity spread, Easter eggs became symbols of the hope of new life through the resurrection of Jesus. Much the way chicks hatch from hard shells, through Easter eggs, Jesus was celebrated as having emerged alive from a stone tomb.

During the Middle Ages, royal families sometimes gave gold-covered eggs as Easter gifts. The most valuable of these eggs were solid gold all the way through. Back then, when folks heard about the hen in "Jack and the Beanstalk" and "The Goose that Laid the Golden Eggs," they thought about kings and queens at Easter time!

People with less money than kings still enjoyed giving eggs as gifts. Easter comes at the end of a religious season called Lent. During the forty days of Lent, most people did not eat eggs.

Victorian photos show enormous, beautifully painted eggs that were taken from ostriches or made of paper mache.

BEST EASTER WISHES

Easter, with its promise bright,
Shed on you its glorious light.

By Easter day, many people were hungry for eggs, for meat, and for all of the sweet foods they had forsaken for forty days. During lent, farmers and housewives saved their eggs. After Lent, they used those eggs for delicious Easter cakes and special foods, as well as for egg hunts and egg games for children.

In parts of Europe and America, children were allowed to parade through neighborhoods singing carols and begging for eggs like trick-or-treaters do for candy today. This was called Easter "pace-egging."

Victorian children loved Easter as much as children do today. Families that could afford to travel and visit relatives often attended church together on Easter morning. They returned for a big holiday dinner of ham or roast lamb, lots of eggs, and hot cross buns for dessert. While aunts and uncles relaxed after the feast, young cousins scoured the yard and garden, racing to see who could find the most eggs. After all of the eggs were found, egg challenges and egg contests would begin.

"The Easter Bunny," captured on a card mailed in 1913.

Various regions of Europe developed distinctive techniques for coloring and decorating eggs. Wonderful examples of egg art were treasured for generations, and some European immigrants brought egg collections to America as heirlooms.

The finest eggs were fragile works of art. They were blown hollow using holes on each end, then kept safe from rough play.

Hard-boiled eggs were preferred for outdoor hunts and games. These eggs were often painted or dyed in bright solid colors, which made them easier to find even in deep grass.

"Easter Egg Rolling, White House Lawn."

During the 1890s, the makers of Lion Coffee inserted free cards into packages of their coffee beans. One of the most popular of their cards was a charming image of "Baby Ruth," released for Easter of 1894. A candy bar was named after this girl, whose mother was famed for her beauty, and whose father was the most powerful politician in America: President Grover Cleveland!

Easter Greeting

Egg tossing games were enjoyed by boys who liked the challenge of catching eggs with their bare hands, with nets, or even in their hats. For a joke, girls would sometimes sneak raw eggs into the toss and then watch for an egg to splat on a boy's face!

Dolley Madison, the wife of President James Madison, loved Easter. She invited children to the Capitol for egg rolling games. In 1878, President Hayes established egg-rolling on the White House lawn as a celebration for the Monday after Easter. The Victorian Easter egg-rolling tradition continues to this day.

Egg rolling contests were more than mere fun; egg rolling represented an important belief that many Victorian parents wanted to teach their children. After Jesus was killed, his body was put into a tomb that was carved like a small cave in the side of a mountain. Soldiers rolled a huge stone in front of the entrance to seal the tomb. On Easter morning, the stone was found rolled aside, and Jesus had escaped the tomb. Victorian egg rolling races helped celebrate the stone that rolled.

Huge eggs made of chicken wire and painted paper mache were popular with Victorians.

Easter
Greetings

Egg Trees

Egg trees became a big fad during the 1890s. Empty egg shells were decorated as ornaments to be hung upon the branches of bushes or little trees. Small egg trees were often placed indoors on tables. This clever tradition first grew famous in Germany, where people wanted to display all of their prettiest Easter eggs so that visitors could enjoy the colors and beauty of all their eggs. Through photos and Easter cards printed in Europe, the egg tree craze quickly spread to America.

This 1909 embossed "Egg Tree" card was printed in Germany to be sold in American card shops.

Victorian Easter

The Colors of Easter

Manufactured dyes became popular during Victorian times. A ten-cent package could change a family's Easter tradition by making it easier for children to join in coloring eggs without having to boil their own dyes from onion skins or toxic plants.

The Diamond Dye company advertised that their egg dyes were also good for making ink, coloring clothes, tinting hat feathers, and even dyeing hair. One 1887 advertising booklet describes how to use their dyes for hand-coloring black and white photographs.

Easter Greetings

Easter's Colors

In some European countries, dark colors were preferred for Easter eggs. Eastern Europeans sometimes even dyed eggs black and placed them on graves. Deep reds were popular in the Ukraine, Greece, Bulgaria, and Romania. Coffee grounds and aged walnut hulls were used to darken homemade dyes.

In Victorian America, yellows were very popular for Easter, partly reflecting a love for chicks, daffodils, and sunrises. Purples symbolized Christ's kingship, because purple dyes were once so expensive that only nobility could afford them. White represented purity.

COPYRIGHTED 1895 BY THE PAAS DYE CO., NEWARK, N.J.

In 1896 Paas Egg Dyes provided six colors per five-cent box. Paas offered a tablet dye that was "an improvement on the old style of dusty powders" and was "free from poison."

Ads for Poor Man's Easter Egg Dyes claimed that a ten-cent package of their five colors would dye six dozen eggs. They said that "Eggs dyed with these colors may be eaten without harm."

Царское жалованіе. (XVI в.)

Fabergé Eggs

Easter morning was more important than Christmas for some Victorians, especially those of the Russian Orthodox faith. A proper celebration included three kisses and an exchange of gift eggs.

As court jeweler to the Russian Czars, Carl Fabergé captured the imagination of the world with his priceless Easter eggs. Each egg held a special "surprise" inside that symbolized the joyful mystery of Easter and the hope of new life that seems hidden at times.

Carl Fabergé began creating jeweled eggs for Czar Alexander III in 1884. The quality and creativity of these eggs was almost beyond imagination. Each one of the over fifty that were made prior to the Russian Revolution is considered a masterpiece. Eggs incorporated diamonds, jasper, and precious stones. Tiny scenes were inside, with replicas of objects like ships, trains, and angels, all crafted from gold and rare gems. Egg themes were kept strictly secret each year until opened by the royal family on Easter morning.

This humorous hand-tinted French photo card depicts a Fabergé style egg with Easter cherubs and a lady "surprise."

Among the legacies of the Victorian age are domestic craft heirlooms of unsurpassed intricacy. Easter eggs from this period remain among the finest ever produced, and breathtaking examples survive representing every technique and tradition of the day. Pysanky eggs were a tradition from the Slavic nations. Eggs were blown hollow and dyed in a base color. Wax was then applied with a stylus in steps of dyeing and wax removal.

Pysanky Easter eggs, like these Russian examples from a century ago, often carried the full saying or the first letters for: "Christ is Risen!"

A century ago, color photography had not yet been perfected. To create artificial color effects, paints and dyes were dabbed or brushed by hand onto black and white photographs. Hand-tinted Easter photos of this type became very popular in Europe and America around 1890, and the fad lasted into the 1920s. Card companies also "faked" color while running cards on traditional printing presses, but their ink choices often differed greatly from the scene's true colors.

Hand-tinted 1911 photo showing decorated goose and ostrich eggs.

Springtime Silliness
Easter Season's Eggs-agerations

Spring can hardly be blamed... it is only natural after cold dark winters that warm sunny days be filled with whimsey, wild play, and "eggs-tra-ordinary" humor.

Long before the Victorians were celebrating Easter with eggs, ancient people joyfully presented spring eggs to Astarte, their goddess of fertility. The Hebrews have used Paschal eggs in their springtime observances of Passover for hundreds of years. And back in the days of medieval kings, gifts of eggs from rich people were happily received by their servants and poor children all throughout Holy Week.

Eggs and springtime have a long history together!

A playful view of a girl "coming out of her shell."

Youthful "eggs-uberance" is captured in a rolling, rollicking 1882 patriotic Easter scene.

Easter Antics

Victorians often found spring to be a saucy flirt: one day warm and coy, the next, cool and threatening. In an age when heating systems produced limited results and when getting around often included exposure to harsh elements, those first perfect days of spring were anticipated more than many of us can imagine.

The Easter season, with its renewal of greens and blooms along favorite paths, inspired celebrations and the wild outdoor revelries of young and old alike... weather permitting!

The outdoor pursuits of a century ago included many of the same sports and activities that we enjoy today, even if the equipment was "old fashioned." Spring was a time to get out the baseball mitt and to dust off the old bicycle seat, same as now.

Early bicyclists, especially the "wheelmen" who dressed in club uniforms and belonged to high-wheeler teams, rode dangerous contraptions with hard rubber tires. At the peak of the 19th-century craze, over 300 companies made bicycles, and Chicago alone boasted some 500 cycle clubs!

Titled "An Easter Souvenir," the flag-waving card to the right captures the rising tide of patriotism that swept through America during the closing decades of the 1800s. Printed in red, white, and blue, symbols of Easter and naval pride are combined in a message celebrating faith in America and our growing "white fleet."

(Opposite) Victorian humor often resorted to sight gags like this, where Easter eggs serve as bicycle wheels.

AN EASTER SOUVENIR.

Victorian Easter

BEST WISHES for EASTER.

"A little chick,
    just hatched to-day,
       My Easter gift to you;
Accept it in
    a kindly way,
       And with my Greeting too."

"God bless thee
      at this time of flowers;
God bless thee
     through life's
        changing hours."

"Accept my Greeting
    on Easter-day,
      May Fortune smile
        on you always."

Ellen Clapsaddle wrote hundreds of light ditties like these for the thousands of Victorian-era greeting cards she illustrated.

Courtships and marriage ceremonies were put on hold during the serious season of Lent. This created many restless couples who eagerly counted down the days to Easter. Stores owned by The Great Atlantic and Pacific Tea Company, later known as "A & P," gave away copies of the above wedding illustration on cards they issued for their 1882 Easter season.

Easter greetings are delivered by a bird "Via Air Mail" in this fanciful card image from 1904.

Striped patterns were often made by wrapping an egg with some kind of tape or band before dyeing. After a color bath, the tape or bands were removed. White designs would remain in all of the areas that had been covered during the dyeing process.

Springtime symbols abound in an outrageous scene of lambs, pussy willows, an Easter rabbit, and an eggshell basket filled with babies. This 1905 card was postmarked Fresno, California.

Eggs that were dyed a solid color could be beautifully enhanced simply by scratching letters, patterns, or scenes through the dye into the shell. Needles were used for creating the thinnest lines on scratch-carved eggs, but knives and nails came in handy for etching bolder lines. The danger was scratching too hard and cracking the shell, so scratch-carved eggs were usually hard boiled. This explains why many Victorian examples never survived — they were eaten, or tossed out when they began to smell!

Saturday afternoon before Easter was a perfect time for children to work on building egg nests for the Easter Rabbit. Gardens and back yards were always preferred, but closets and corners inside would serve if the weather was bad.

Along with the natural world, the spirit of Victorian families reawakened each spring as Easter preparations were excitedly made. Children would fall asleep late, their imaginations stirred with fantasies and dreams of the wondrous adventures that might greet them on Easter morn.

Easter Greetings.

"There's no excuse for feeling sad
    On Easter,
    So I need scarcely say "Be glad'
    On Easter;

But still I pray the day may bring
    Into your heart the smile of Spring
And then with all the world you'll sing
    On Easter."

— Card signed: "Your Sister Mary, Easter Sunday, April 12, 1914."

"On Easter morn,
    when you arise,
        May sunshine greet
            your smiling eyes;
And may its
    radiance
        with you stay
    Till every mist
        is burned away."

(Opposite) Artificial eggs were used for lighthearted effects in many Victorian studio photographs. Oversized eggs were created from newspaper and paste, from wood, or even from cloth stretched over wire. A seam is clearly visible on the egg held in this hand-tinted photo.

4304
COPYRIGHTED 1907 BY JULIUS BIEN & CO. N.Y.

EASTER GREETINGS

Easter Greetings

Easter Greetings

"Bunnies greet you
    they've come to say
        'I wish you well
            this Easter Day.'"

"I'm glad this
    Easter rabbit's ear
        Is long and wide,
            so he can hear
The many
    greetings
        that I send
To you
    my little friend."

"May the bunnies and chicks
    of Easter Day
        Scatter gladness on your way."

—from three Victorian cards

Easter Greetings

Victorian humor sometimes seems bizarre by today's standards. Dressed in fuzzy yellow, spring chicks romp in a strange game where one girl peeks out of an egg peephole.

"Peep-hole" Easter eggs really did exist! (See the example on page 24.) People often cooked homemade sugar eggshells rather than trying to cut window peepholes from actual chicken eggs. Sugar eggshells were made in two halves that were bonded together with icing after the tiny scene inside was painstakingly completed.

Happy Easter-Tide

Mother.

Like eggs and flower bulbs, small pussy willow buds symbolize new life that is ready to burst forth. Pussy willows grow heartily in the wetlands of much of the Northern Hemisphere. Because pussy willows are so abundant at springtime, some Victorians used them instead of palm fronds on Palm Sunday, or even as substitutes for vases of lilies on Easter morning.

Victorian artists loved to comically exaggerate, as in this egg painting illustration from 1908.

Beautiful eggs were treasured... if not eaten! Children were taught how to make hollow eggs by poking a hole into each end and blowing the insides into a bowl.

For homemade egg dyes, yellow was boiled from onion skins, apple bark, and goldenrod flowers. Red dyes came from red onion skins and beets. Green dyes were made from spinach and moss. Blues were the most difficult to make. Some people used huckleberries, but others boiled blue dye out from old blue clothes they no longer needed.

Easter Greetings.

Some people used to carry one big special egg with them to their Easter Sunday worship service. When they met someone else who had an egg, they would tap their eggs together and say, "Christ is risen!" The proper Easter reply was: "Yes! He is risen indeed!"

Victorian Easter

Whimsical Victorian Easter cards are found depicting eggs as clever substitutes for everything from bicycle wheels to colorful raindrops. Chicks frolic in many of these springtime scenes, often appearing anthropomorphically as children, or sometimes just as cute little birds.

In other card scenes, chicks and children trade places, but with the children taking the roles of the chicks! The most common examples show a young boy or girl hatching from an egg.

"An Easter Dream"

Springtime silliness rises to new heights in one comical 1911 scene where eggs and bubbles confuse everyone, including the mother hen.

(Opposite) Victorian egg games may have inspired "An Easter Dream," published in 1894. (The red eggs seem to be the "bad eggs" in this dream!) In addition to egg tossing, egg spinning and egg rolling, children competed in egg croquet and egg tapping, where children knocked each other's eggs together until only the strongest egg remained.

Joyful Easter

Once again
the
Joyous Season
with its greetings
and
its mirth

Once again
its gay
good wishes
and its blossoms
o'er
the earth

Easter Blessings

From Bulbs to Easter Blooms

Like fuzzy yellow chicks or fluffy new-born bunnies, the first flowers of spring declare to all who listen: the season of new life has arrived! During the cold dark times of winter, hard brown bulbs wait for their day to stir, to rise, and to bloom. Then, often the very week of Easter, flowers burst open to greet the returning light and warmth of spring. For Victorians, the bulbs of lilies, daffodils, and tulips represented Christ's tomb, and new blossoms symbolized resurrection from death.

Celebrating New Life
Springtime Chicks, Blooms and Children

Loving Easter Greetings

Easter was a holiday dedicated to the celebration of new life, even in the barnyard!

Arise my heart and sing thy Easter song, To the great anthem of returning bird,
And sweetening bud and green ascending blade, Add thou thy word."

—*Easter card, copyright 1910*

Apart from Easter, cultures around the world have long valued activities honoring the return of spring. Special foods, spring bonfires, and celebrations for new-born animals were all widely observed.

The name "Easter" is ancient. It comes from the word "east," and it relates to the sun, sunrises, and pagan religions that had gods with names like Austron and Eostre. Like Christians, people of these religions longed for renewal and the rejuvenation of life.

As the Christian faith spread in Europe, sensitive local leaders were often creative in helping communities make

RELIABLE INCUBATOR AND BROODER CO.
QUINCY, ILL.

PAT'D AUG. 18, 1885.

the transition into a Christian world view.

Rather than abandoning all of the holidays and festival traditions of each region, leaders encouraged people to redefine what it was that they were celebrating. For example, chicken eggs that were once offered to a pagan goddess to insure fertility began to be dyed red to honor the blood of Christ, and Easter eggs were reaffirmed, but as symbols of Christ's tomb.

Beautifully embossed Easter cards were common, but ones like this with real silk embellishments were very special.

Victorian Easter

Chicks gleefully chirp Easter Carols in a humorous 1911 sunrise scene. The chicks are shown in front of Easter Lilies that were largely unknown by Victorians before the 1870s. For centuries prior to the "discovery" and importation of these exotic Trumpet Lilies from Japan, the white narcissus of the Alps was the most popular Easter bloom. Victorians liked how the shape of Japan's lilies reminded them of how they imagined joyful music sounding forth from an angel's trumpet.

"May the blossoms

of Easter

rejoice your eye,

The sunshine

of Easter

brighten your sky;

May the hope

of Easter

delight your heart,

The Joy

of Easter

ne'er

from you depart."

—Card mailed in 1906

Victorian Easter

"I wish you joy — but oh, instead of this cold, formal greeting,
   Much more, I wish, this Easter Day, That you and I were meeting."
                                        —Victorian Easter card

Victorian Easter

Easter Greeting

Dear flowers, how did you know
'Twas time to bloom?
"Dear child" the Master cries,
"Ye shall arise."

The miracles of fresh buds and spring blooms have long stirred hope that blessings await those who persist in faith.

A happy EASTER

"Now Songbirds call,
      and green leaves
            break,
In all the
      countryside,
May gladness wake
      for you and make
A happy
      Easter tide."
—Victorian Easter card

BEST EASTER WISHES

Pussy Willows for Easter Play

People living from England all the way to Russia have long cherished the role of pussy willows in their Easter celebrations. Also known outside of America as "goat willows," children picked them for parades, games, and flower arrangements. Young adults picked them for "switching" on the day after Easter, when flirting men would tap young women with a branch on the pretext of wishing them blessings and health. Such branches were called "the rod of life," and they were often decorated by Victorians with ribbons and flowers.

Victorian Easter

"Let all
new life
tender
and true
Speak of
the risen
Christ
to you."
—Victorian
Easter card

Easter Greetings

"You ought to see my little lambs. They are so cute and just run and play all the time. They chase me all over."

— *from card below, dated April 5, 1909.*

A JOUYOUS EASTER

"Now voices of the coming spring
    Are ringing far and wide,
I pray that they to you may bring,
    A Happy Eastertide."

"Happiness with you abide
All this joyful Easter-tide,

And when its glad hours depart
Leave its peace within your heart."

—Easter card, dated 1910

A Joyful EASTER.

Springtime romance is celebrated in a Victorian Easter image depicting two chicks slyly stealing kisses beneath an umbrella. The joys of youth and the exuburance of the season are reinforced by fresh apple blossoms and a discarded top hat.

"My simple greeting take,
May joy with you abide,
And bright life's pathway make,
For you this Easter-tide."

"Were I a flower, on Easter day,
I'd bloom my best, for you;
I'd scent the air and store away
My honey for you, too."

Victorian Easter

A Happy Eastertide

"Oh, look who's here!"

"Look Who's Here!"

The Easter Hare tradition was greatly enjoyed by Germans, who popularized their fun celebrations in America during Victorian times. Rabbits are much more common in America than hares, so his named was changed to Easter Rabbit. German parents encouraged children to make nests for eggs on Easter Eve. Sometimes on Easter morning, bunnies would be spotted hopping near nests filled with dyed eggs, and that helped children believe that the magical stories of the Easter Rabbit were really true!

The Easter Bunny
Holiday Hares Joyfully A-Bounding

A child enchants a rabbit and her other wee friends by singing sunrise carols in 1891.

Victorian holiday celebrations usually included religious activities for adults, but parents wanted children to experience the wonder of the day as well. For children, little could beat the thrill of finding the Easter Bunny's treasures on Easter morning.

Rabbit Cards

"What sweet Easter Cards,"
the Grandmother said,
and she took the bright gifts
which Charlie and Fred,
as they joyfully
climbed on her knees
held up to view.
"We had presents galore,"
she said, "but the cards
in the dear days of yore
were never so
pretty as these."
"See this rabbit," said Fred,
as he held up a card
which he viewed
with a loving
and tender regard...

—From 1890s unsigned poem

On What Date
Do Bunnies Arrive?

Because Easter Rabbits were viewed by Victorians as lighthearted symbols of spring and joy, bunnies were not supposed to arrive until after Lent, on Easter Eve during Holy Saturday celebrations at the very earliest. But upon which spring Saturday was Easter Eve?

Easter is celebrated each year on a different Sunday between March 22 and April 25. The spring equinox, when daylight and darkness are equal in length, happens around March 21. In A.D. 325 the Council of Nicaea said Easter should fall on the first Sunday following the first full moon after vernal equinox.

Victorian Easter

Teaching rabbits to behave during Easter lessons is no easy trick! The back of this 1893 illustration reads: "These Beautiful Easter Greetings are to be had only in the one pound packages of Lion Coffee between Feb. 10th and Easter Sunday."

(Opposite) This 1909 Easter greeting was mailed to Florida from a teenage girl in Iowa.

Many ancient cultures used hares as springtime symbols for the moon and fertility because hares like to eat in moonlight, and because hares are known for having many babies each spring. Although jackrabbits are actually hares, America has mostly rabbits. Rabbits can live 10 years and can have as many as six litters for up to 50 babies per year!

The small hares of Palestine are only mentioned twice in the Bible. There is no early Christian symbolism associated with hares or Easter Rabbits.

Hares run 35 miles per hour!

Long ago, spring bonfires were sometimes called "Rabbit Fires." Parents told children the fires were from rabbits boiling Easter eggs!

"May we know the rest this Easter
  Of the Father's loving care,
May we thank the One who gives us
  Each the right, that love to share."
  — Victorian Easter card

Fancy egg-shaped trinket and candy boxes were popular with Victorians who wanted to give a special token of affection for Easter. Adding eggs like these to an Easter basket would make memories for a lifetime.

Some of the finest egg keepsakes of the 19th century were painted, not dyed. Artistic gift eggs were made of china, wood, or solid glass. Such eggs are highly sought after by collectors today.

Easter Bells

Easter bells echoed over the Victorian countryside every spring. Back before everyone owned clocks and watches, churches used their bells to announce the time of day. At noon, church bells would ring twelve times. When bells rang loudly for more than twelve times, people knew there was an emergency... or a big celebration like Easter sunrise! Easter bells were especially welcomed because they ended the season of Lent, and also because even farm dinner bells were kept silent all during Holy Week just before Easter.

Easter Greetings

Fashionably dressed like the popular Buster Brown comic strip hero of his day, this Victorian boy shares an egg with the Easter Bunny in a 1910 greeting card scene. Short-eared Easter Rabbits like this are America's version of Europe's Easter Hare.

Easter cards were often printed in Germany, so many show a long-eared "Oster Haas."

Green Eggs and Lent Season

Green eggs were special in Germany. People were not supposed to eat meat or eggs during Lent. They could break the rule on Green Thursday, but only if they boiled their eggs in spinach to dye them green.

The word Lent comes from "lengthening," for how days grow longer in the springtime. Lent starts on Ash Wednesday and lasts for the 40 days (not counting Sundays) until Easter.

"Mardi Gras" is French for "Fat Tuesday." People were encouraged to eat up all of their sweet and greasy foods on that day before Lent started.

Two European Easter Hares bring a moment of playful magic to a girl out egg hunting in the woods in her new Easter bonnet.

During Lent, people remember how Jesus suffered for 40 days while he was in the desert, and they think about his death.

The mood changes on Easter, when people think about new life. In Europe, the Easter Hare symbolized the joy of turning from sad days to times of happy celebration.

A Joyful Eastertide

"May this Easter shed
  a fragrant beauty
O'er many a day
  of dull and cheerless duty
And light thy wintry way."
    — Victorian Easter card

The back of this lovely card reads:

"Dear Cousin Ruth,
    How many eggs will you eat
to-morrow?
    Come over and tell us when
you can.
    Wish you all a happy Easter.
    Your loving Cousin."
—New York, April 15, 1911

An all-American rabbit proudly guards his red, white, and blue eggs.

Brer Rabbit was as loved by children a century ago as Winnie the Pooh is today. In fact, Brer Rabbit's success probably helped create audiences for Beatrix Potter's Peter Rabbit (launched in 1902), as well as for A.A. Milne's Pooh Bear (first in 1926).

Comical ballroom bunny images of a Brer Rabbit style were used in the 1880s to help promote "Luncheon Beef" packaged by the Armour Packing Company of Kansas City.

Brer Rabbit rose to fame through Joel Chandler Harris' "Uncle Remus" stories that were based upon old plantation folktales and slave stories. Early Brer Rabbit illustrations were like these dancing rabbit images, except with farming clothes.

BEST
EASTER WISHES

To bear an Easter wish from me,
I choose a tiny craft, you see;
I trust Brer Rabbit just the same,
And send my wish by
                    Monoplane.

LUNCHEON BEEF.
·READY·FOR·TABLE·USE·

The first collection of Uncle Remus stories was published in 1880. It sold 10,000 copies within four months. These two flying Brer Rabbit Easter cards date from 1912.

Victorian Easter

(Opposite) Dreams of springtime and
Easter Rabbits fill an 1893 illustration.

Bunnies will eat almost any kind of plant,
including Easter Pussy Willows if nobody is
looking! Victorians loved pet rabbits; they would
even buy them fancy collars and let them hop
around indoors.

A Happy Easter

The Gift of Life

Girls in new Easter bonnets and white dresses show off a pet Cottontail Rabbit in a 1910 greeting mailed from North Dakota. Furry young bunnies and fuzzy yellow chicks were popular as Easter gifts, and many middle-class Victorian families had a rabbit hutch or a chicken coop in the back yard.

Cottontail Rabbits, with their white splash of fur beneath their tails, are native to America and are found in almost every state. Long ago, Cottontails were unknown in Europe, home of the original Easter Hare.

Victorian Easter

"Here comes Peter Cottontail,
Hoppin' down the bunny trail,
Hippity hoppity,
Easter's on its way."

These lines were popularized
by singer Gene Autry in 1949,
almost fifty years after the
card to the right was mailed
from Oklahoma. After Autry's
hit song, Peter Cottontail was
firmly established as a sort of
Easter Santa, a bunny who
would be: "Bringin' ev'ry girl
and boy, A basketful of Easter
joy, Things to make your
Easter Bright and gay."

EASTER
GREETINGS.

Springtime Fantasies
Easter Fairies, Wee Folk and Magic

Greetings

So Santa Claus needed little helpers to handle Christmas, so it was believed by many that the Easter Rabbit used Wee Folk helpers to deliver eggs on Easter Eve. Some children imagined gnomes riding with sacks of eggs on the backs of bouncing bunnies. Others imagined fairy angels magically whisking the eggs through the air. However imagined, such fantasies fueled the magic of Easter morning!

Victorian Easter

Magical Wee Folk helped distribute Victorian Easter eggs according to many fanciful illustrations. Gnomes and angel fairies seemed to enjoy the work

    . . . most of the time!

Victorian Easter

"Each dainty blossom of the Spring
   Each bud upon the spray,
Sweet message for Easter bring
   To one and all to-day.
I send you this card
   to confide
My wishes to you this
   Easter-tide.
—Greeting from Connecticut,
1913

EASTER
GREETING

By bunny airship
line
I send this little elf
To carry you the
EASTER thought
I cannot bring myself.

"A Happy Easter"

Fairy angel girls deliver an enormous Easter egg in a 1908 hand-tinted photo from Kansas.

"Let all things seen and unseen, Their notes of gladness blend,
For Christ the Lord is risen, Our Joy that hath no end."   —1910 Easter Greeting

Victorian Easter

"Green Thursday" dates back to the Middle Ages, when priests carried green plants on this day of Holy Week just before Easter. Church people who wanted forgiveness also carried green sprigs on this day, and everybody ate green foods like spinach, herb soups, and salads.

Some superstitious people believed that if you refused to eat a green plant on Green Thursday, then you would magically turn into something bad like a donkey! Many Victorians still observed Green Thursday.

Fantasy Wee Folk images and wild folk tales of Br'er Rabbit were so popular around the turn-of-the-century that they even began making appearances on Easter Egg Tree ornaments. The following comes from a Victorian article:

Easter Greetings

"The tree was an evergreen and, instead of a Santa Claus or fairy at the top of the tree, 'Br'er Bunny' had the post of honor.... Eggshells were painted and finished up to represent clowns, brownies, and gnomes."

—Mother's Magazine, 1906

Swedish Easter cards often show witches. Long ago, some people believed that witches hated churches, so during Holy Week witches would fly to church bell towers to create trouble. For fun, some Swedish girls dressed as "Easter hags."

Påett ägg jag till Blåkulla far
För att önska dig en Påsk så rar!

Glad Påsk

S. Sundius-Dahlström

EASTER GREETINGS

In Swedish folklore, Easter hags rose up their chimneys and flew to a dark haunted place called "Blåkulla," where they congregated for a witches sabbath with fairies, gnomes, trolls, and the devil.

Celebrating With Style
Hats and Fashionable Traditions

BUY YOUR
EASTER GLOVES
AT
FREAR'S TROY BAZAAR.
EVERY PAIR WARRANTED.

This ad for Easter gloves dates from the early 1880s. The postcard below was mailed in Connecticut in 1913.

AN EASTER

WISH

Easter

The tradition of dressing up for Easter goes back many hundreds of years. In the Middle Ages, new converts to Christianity were baptized in fresh white robes on Easter, and everyone else dressed in the best clothes they owned. After the service, the entire village would parade through the region, praying and singing hymns at each place they stopped.

I WISH I HAD AN EASTER HAT,
WITH ROSES 'ROUND THE CROWN,
A LITTLE BOW UPON THE TOP,
AND STRINGS TO TIE IT DOWN.

Nothing could communicate Victorian grace and celebration quite like a new hat for Easter.

"Fain I'd write a dainty sonnet
    To my lady's Easter bonnet,
Though 'twere plain with nothing on it,
    She'd adorn it when she dons it."
—Victorian Easter card

Best Wishes for
A Happy Easter

Before Easter morning's sunshine, the final cool wet days of winter were frequently filled with craftsy indoor projects. In addition to preparing egg trees, bunny baskets, and Easter feasts, mothers and daughters often spent late hours embellishing their new bonnets for a joyful Sunday sunrise debut. Affordable hats were frequently upgraded into lavish creations of ribbons, laces, blooms, embroideries and bows.

Easter chocolates and jelly beans were Victorian favorites. Jelly beans were made from a form of Turkish Delight confection that was coated with sugar and syrup in a process called panning. Egg-shaped jelly beans came in boxes or were sold as "penny candy" from fancy glass jars.

Fashionable Easter Foods

A MERRY EASTER

Traditional Easter feasts often included lamb or ham, eggs, and some kind of baked treat like hot cross buns or pretzels.

Hot cross buns are spicy with raisins. They are topped with white icing shaped like a cross.

Pretzels were first created by fifth-century monks in Rome, who baked them during Lent to give to the poor as bread. Pretzel in Latin means "little arms." An old-fashioned pretzel turned horizontally appears to have arms folded upwards in prayer.

Glossary

Brer Rabbit: Fictional rabbit from Uncle Remus stories, hugely popular after 1880s. (88, 89, 102)

Easter Bonnets, Hats, Fashion: Fancy clothes worn on Easter Sunday. (104-107)

Easter Colors: Purple, Red, White, Green, Yellow, Blue. (12, 28, 52, 61)

Easter: Religious holiday when Victorians celebrated their faith and the joys of spring; often included special church services recalling Jesus' resurrection from a tomb. Related to the words "east" and "Eostre." See: Passover, Pesach, Pasha, Paaske, etc. (see especially 35, 60, 75)

Easter Eggs: Symbols for new life, springtime, and the tomb of Jesus. (10, 16, 17, 21, 25, 61)

Easter Foods: Hot cross buns, eggs, roast lamb, jelly beans, pretzels, etc. (19, 20, 108, 109)

Easter Lilies: Trumpet Lilies imported from Japan via Bermuda after 1870s. (4, 5, 6, 58, 62)

Easter-Tide or Eastertide: The season around Easter, often including the week after Easter.

Easter Sunrise: Special time for worship and celebration on Easter Sunday. (14, 15, 53)

Egg Contests, Egg Rolling: Spring festival games using hard boiled eggs. (16-25, 44, 53, 57, 72)

Egg Dyes and Decorating: Traditions for preparing Easter eggs. (26-33, 42, 43, 47, 49, 52)

Easter Rabbit, Hare: Ancient animal associated with spring, fertility, and Easter. (44, 72-93)

Egg Trees: Like Christmas trees, but for Easter with eggs as ornaments. (26, 102)

Fabergé Eggs: Priceless jeweled eggs with tiny scenes made for Russian Czars. (30, 31)

Good Friday: Day of Holy Week recalling Jesus' death on a cross and burial in a tomb.

Gnomes and Easter Fairy Angels: Wee folk who helped the Easter Rabbit bring eggs. (94-103)

Holy Week: From Palm Sunday to Easter Sunday recalling the death and resurrection of Jesus.

Lamb: Easter symbol reflecting belief that Jesus's blood served like a lamb's sacrifice. (11)

Lent: Forty days (excluding Sundays) from Ash Wednesday to Easter. (8, 18, 19, 41, 81, 84, 85)

Maundy Thursday: Day of Holy Week recalling the Last Supper before Christ was betrayed. "Maundy" is from Latin for "commandment," the law from Jesus to love one another. (8)

Pace-Egging: Like trick-or-treating, but children begging for eggs. (19)

Palm Sunday: First day of Holy Week, recalling Jesus' arrival in Jerusalem. (8)

Pascha – Paaske: "Pascha" is the Greek word for Easter, coming from the Hebrew *Pesach.* *Paaske* is Norwegian, *Paques* is French, *Pask* is Swedish, *Pascua* is Spanish, etc.

Passover – Pesach: "Pesach" is the old Hebrew word for Passover, the festival when Jews recall the angel of death in Egypt passing over homes marked by the blood of a lamb. (9, 11, 35)

Peter Cottontail: Easter Rabbit made famous by Gene Autry's 1949 song, with his name drawn from Beatrix Potter's two rabbits, Peter and Cotton-tail, created in 1902. (93)

Pussy Willows: Popular spring plant used in Easter celebrations. (50, 66, 91)

Victorian: Refers to the era of Queen Victoria, who ruled from 1837-1901. In common usage it describes the prevailing values, behaviors and styles from the 1870s to about 1915.

DAVE CHEADLE has a masterful knowledge of history, religion, and the Victorian era. He has authored over 150 articles and six books, including *Victorian Angels, Victorian Fairies, Arctic Obsession: the Victorian Race for the North Pole*, and the definitive book on the subject, *Victorian Trade Cards: Historical Reference & Value Guide*. He co-founded The Advertising Trade Card Collector's Association and was founding editor of *The Advertising Trade Card Quarterly*.

Cheadle has a degree in Philosophy and Religion, with advanced graduate work in History and Literature. He is married with two children and is pastor of Harvest Christian Community, in Wheat Ridge, Colorado.

Visit: www.VictorianEaster.org